WHEN YOUR CHILD NEEDS A HUG

Larry Losoncy

ABBEY PRESS
St. Meinrad, Indiana 47577

TO MY PARENTS,
Joseph and Rose Losoncy,
and to my parents-in-law,
Harold and Lois Sibley.

PHOTO CREDITS: Camerique, Cover; Bob Smith/Laura Garza, page 6; Randy Dieter, page 19; Rick Smolan, page 27; Paul Conklin, page 36; Wallowitch, page 47; Florence Sharp, page 58; Kay Freeman, page 64; Jean Claude Lejeune, page 73; H. Crane, Essey Enterprises, page 88

Library of Congress Catalog Card Number
78-73016
ISBN: 0-87029-141-6

©1978 St. Meinrad Archabbey
St. Meinrad Indiana 47577

CONTENTS

Foreword   4

I Emotional Development

Chapter One: **Infancy**   7

Chapter Two: **Childhood**   22

Chapter Three: **Adolescence**   37

II The Parent's Role

Chapter Four: **When to Hug Infants**   51

Chapter Five: **When to Hug Children**   65

Chapter Six: **When to Hug Adolescents**   76

III Everyone's Role in Her/His Own Emotional Development

Chapter Seven: **When to Hug the Kid that Lives within Each of Us**   89

Suggestions for Further Reading   94

FOREWORD

When Your Child Needs A Hug is a book about the emotional development of children and some of the many things parents can do to help that development along. In writing it, I feel guilty and inadequate: guilty at all the times I have not hugged my children when they needed hugging; inadequate in the face of many similar failures I know will occur in the future. I am not a perfect parent! Neither are you. The abiding cross of parenthood is that we will never be perfect. But thank God, we cannot be perfect, for if it were truly possible to be perfect parents, our judgement for falling short would be too severe to bear.

The message of this little book is one of understanding, patience, and affection. Emotional development from infancy through adolescence is described in the first three chapters. Some ideas about how to help our children grow and develop in healthy ways during these same periods of life are given in the next three chapters for hugs come in many different forms. The final chapter proposes how we can hug ourselves.

The nice thing about being parents is that our children love us and grow up to be good people most of the time. We need to hug them all the time. That way, guilt and inadequacy give way to warmth and strength. God does not call us to be perfect parents, but to love our children.

CHAPTER ONE: Infancy

This is a book about the emotional development of children. "Child" means at least three different things today. In one meaning, to be a child is to be the offspring of our parents. In this sense, a child can be a person of any age. "Child" also refers, in transactional analysis language, to that dimension of personality in which feelings are dominant. In this sense persons of all ages are part child. All of us often let our feelings take over, be they playful, rebellious, or otherwise.

The third sense in which "child" is used today is that in which "childhood" means a stage in life. Developmental psychologists generally see three stages of development before adulthood: infancy (first six years of life), childhood (next six years), and adolescence (approximately ages twelve through eighteen). In the very loosest sense, all three of the stages preceding adulthood could be called childhood. In that sense infants, children, and teenagers are children, and in that sense this book will take up the emotional development of children from birth through the mid-teens.

Rather than talk about development in generalities, we will break the discussion down by ages. Babies will be considered as thirty months old and younger; infants will be considered as people in the two year to six year old range; children will be considered as people in the years from seven through twelve; adolescence will be considered as those in their teens.

There is no one set way to classify people for purposes of discussion. Whether classification is attempted by age or by development, each author tends to develop his or her own reasons for classifying differently from some other author's point of view. I offer these age breakdowns from the standpoint of convenience and experience. I think that it is convenient to consider babies in the first thirty months of their life as being in a special category of age and development, a category which ends approximately when they are walking and beginning to talk. The next classification, thirty months to six years, coincides roughly with the preschool years and ends when the strongest dependencies of infants are also ending. Childhood, the years between infancy and adolescence, is also a convenient classification since these are the elementary school years.

Babies

Lucie Barber, a mother and researcher on the

staff of the Union Character Research Project, has published a detailed description of how babies develop in certain respects. Lucie is one of this nation's authorities on the subject, and she works as part of a project which has been observing and reporting human development during the early part of life for more than forty years. Most of what is said here about babies will rely on her work.

From the time of birth, development is evident in everything that babies are, or have, or do. For simplicity, and at the cost of neatness, we will discuss much of this development in terms simply of what it "centers around," (a rough and ready but direct and clear approach). We will discuss development as it evidences itself in 1) mouth-eyes (functioning almost as an integral unit), 2) manipulation (fine muscle skills), 3) language, and 4) motor ability (gross muscle skills). While these "developments" (1-4) are not emotional development as such, they very much affect 5) emotional and 6) social development. The interrelation among all six is shown in tabular form on pages 12 and 13.

Mouth development is essential for life in the newborn, while eye development makes life interesting. By two months, babies can not only suck very well, they can pause in their sucking and rest a bit; their swallowing has improved, and they can follow the movement of bright objects such as those of a mobile above the bed. These developments begin to bring a *sense of enjoyment*, which is important for good emotional life. By four months, babies can suck both for nourishment and just for the sheer fun of it. They can reach out and grasp what they see. By seven months they can keep their eyes on an object all the way from the time they see it until it arrives safely in their mouth. By the end of the first year they can gnaw or chew. By thirty months their eye development improves to the point of being able to study people, play simple games, and pay attention to distant objects.

Emotional security begins to build up in proportion to how well the baby can see, enjoy, and control the world. The most important aspect of the world at this age, of course, is food. Control of eating hinges on muscle, mouth, and eye development. By thirty months, the eyes and mouth have developed enough to make eating a joy. Muscle development, both fine and gross motor skills, has also kept pace.

Muscle development, for example, by thirty months, has gone forward sufficiently for the baby to grasp and release things such as spoons and forks; drinking from a cup has become easy; staying with things until they are finished has become a challenge, so that the baby likes to eat until the food is all gone. By this age babies enjoy picking up pieces of cereal one piece at a time and eating each piece. By this time also the baby is able to climb, walk, run, turn doorknobs, explore, and generally range about. Emotional advances in terms of security are again the result, since the baby is able to control his eating, find food, and also explore and begin to take charge of his world.

Language and social development also take place at a rapid pace during these early months. Since our emotional life and development are greatly helped by interacting with people around us, language and social development directly affect emotional development. By two months of age, babies have several varieties of crying. By four months they cry for what they want. By sixteen months they try to influence people with words and gestures. They are interacting with people, developing social skills and games such as hide and seek, and imitating coughing, nose-blowing, sneezing. By thirty months they have a good sense of what is theirs and what belongs to others.

To sum up, development of mouth-eyes, manipulation, language, and motor abiblity skills helps emotional development right from the beginning. A great deal of emotional development is going on during infancy. Babies are not just lying around vegetating! By two months, babies have developed a strong sense of trust. By four months they have begun to learn to control anger and to take emotional delight and express it by laughing, squealing, smiling. By seven months their curiosity has developed to the point that they enjoy learning about things and can sense the emotional moods of others. Frustration has also been experienced and has been met with tears and worry. By one year of age, babies can sense and enjoy loving protection; they are beginning to identify when people are angry and afraid. Very soon jealousy sets in, as well as the need and ability to control jealousy and do unpleasant things, which is self-control. By two years of age, babies are trying hard to please others, have a sense of home, safety, confidence, and an emotional life of their own which includes ups and downs. By thirty months they are beginning to cope with fears of specific things such as dogs, thunder, and the toilet. They are anxious to help and to perform duties of their own.

Developmental Stages of Children

months	MOUTH-EYES	MANIPULATION (Small Muscle)	LANGUAGE
1 and 2	Sucks, swallows, pauses. Eyes follow large objects.	Thrashes arms and reaches.	Communicates pain.
3 and 4	Sucks for eating, leisure. Grasps what is seen. Shows color preference.	Retrieves items, develops thumb-forefinger pinch.	Loves being talked to; babbles; facially expresses anger, fear and joy.
5 to 7	Keeps eyes on object all the way to mouth. Likes to look in mirror.	Develops skill in eye-hand coordination. Visually guides reaching. Accepts one object at a time.	Practices vowel sounds and repeats sounds.
8 to 12	Chews, gnaws and drinks from cup. Is interested in location and movement.	Reaches, grasps and retrieves. Enjoys picking up small objects.	Utters two syllables, like "mama." Intones sounds.
13 to 16	Closes eyes and still gets object in mouth. Leans and judges landing.	Eats from a spoon, left and right handed. Shows persistence.	Uses words and gestures to influence people.
17 to 24	Tries to do everything at once. Up becomes interesting. Studies people.	Masters drinking from a cup. Masters release. Takes off shoes, hat, mittens. Unzips zippers.	Pays attention to sentences & how one speaks: kindly, clearly, loudly.
25 to 30	Develops table manners.	Tries to write and copies things.	Begins to speak in sentences.

1 to 30 Months

MOTOR (Large Muscle)	EMOTIONAL	SOCIAL
Is a random uncoordinated mass of activity by long muscles: legs, arms, back.	Is trusting, finds music soothing. Vents a great deal.	Smiles, recognizes family, responds to social contact.
Holds head steady, has hand control, pushes self to standing position.	Takes emotional delight, laughs, smiles, squeals. Fusses when tired or hungry.	Responds to voices, turns head to see people, notices strangers.
Rolls, sits, stands. Has a sense of purpose in reaching and creeping to objects.	Shows curiosity by wrinkling forehead, tensing face muscles & opening mouth.	Distinguishes friends, angry voices, strangers. Enjoys self in mirror.
Pokes, probes, pushes. Likes to put things together.	Has ups and downs. Has a new fear of strangers. Is able to reconcile.	Begins to be able to overcome fear and anger.
Tries hard to walk, play & go for forbidden objects.	Identifies when people are angry or afraid. Can be jealous. Smiles when useful.	Interacts with people. Likes hide & seek. Pulls hair. Plays games.
Controls gross body movement, runs, turns doorknobs. Begins toilet training.	Is sensitive to adult approval, often over-responsive, and is quite assertive.	Imitates others. Expands own sense of world. Likes to blow out matches.
Develops bladder control. Gives guests tours of home. Stoops and squats.	Begins to cope with fears of dogs, toilet, etc.	Is aggressive: claiming, taking, achieving ownership.

These developments are rapid and widespread within each baby. They set the stage, so to speak, for even more dramatic emotional development during the next few years, development which goes on in all the ways already mentioned here but which becomes especially important in terms of the baby's *self-concept* or *self-image,* the most important factor of all in emotional development for the rest of the baby's life.

Infants and Self-Regard: Years Two through Six

Self-regard for Lucie Barber and John Peatling, as well as others of their co-workers at the Character Research Project, is another term for self-concept and self-image. It is made up of numerous identifiable components, the most important of which are:

> Purposeful learning of skills,
> Completing tasks,
> Coping with fears,
> Responding to requests,
> Dealing with frustrations,
> Acquiring socially acceptable behavior,
> Developing imagination in play.

Barber and Peatling have created materials by which parents are able to quickly and easily determine how far their children have matured in these areas along a measurement from very immature to very mature.

Infants, from about two to six years of age, can be observed to mature in all seven of these aspects, which taken together constitute important components of self-image and, for that reason, determine emotional development.

Purposeful learning of skills begins without any clear pattern. Infants at about age two begin learning the names of things such as colors. They learn how to draw lines and how to go up and down stairs. Their learning is stop and go, erratic, inconsistent. They will often start a new task before the first one is finished, for instance trying to put on a shoe before they have finished dressing, or starting to hop into bed before they have finished taking off their shoes and socks. At the very mature end of learning new skills, children practice in order to be prepared, knowing that what they are practicing will be helpful in the future. Examples include children watering seeds every day so that a plant will sprout, practicing on their bicycles so that they will get good at riding them, practicing going to school or other places with adults so that they will get experienced enough to go by themselves.

In between the two extremes of immature and very mature lies a great deal of growth and development which will take three or four years for each child to achieve. The three major steps in this process are: the "imitate and repeat" stage, the "me do it" stage, and a stage of accepting coaching and help. Learning skills is a way in which infants begin to take control of themselves and of their world. That is to say, it is the beginning of acquiring power, self reliance, security.

Completing tasks begins at the immature level of not sticking with any task, no matter how simple; it proceeds to the very mature six-year-old level of sticking with even very complex tasks and

The Components of Self-Regard

finishing what was begun. In between are, once again, three recognizable levels of increased maturity, the first of which is beginning to stay with simple tasks especially if done with a parent or adult, then completing tasks without supervision, and then working well at more complex tasks. In their development of task completion, infants are learning perseverance and the stick-to-itive qualities of patience, application, and determination: qualities which like all other character traits and emotions are learned rather than inherited or genetically determined.

Coping with fears is a trait that requires cultivation from an almost zero starting point. Infants are almost completely dependent on parents for reassurance and safety. Unable to understand their fears, and helpless in the face of them, they can respond only by crying for help, getting close to mother, hiding. Things which they may find terrifying include loud noises, the dark, animals, strangers. At the very mature end of the continuum children can cope with fears independently of their parents, using their own understanding, strategies, and skills.

In between these extremes are three stages of increasing maturity: beginning to cope with familiar fears, coping when given reassurance, and coping when given explanations. At first, infants begin to identify the source of some of their familiar fears such as the vacuum cleaner, Dad's power saw, the mailman. Instead of screaming or clinging in terror they try to cope. Later still, they will want to be brave and try to be brave but they will still need some help and reassurance, such as holding a parent's hand or wanting to stand close to a parent. Stand on the beach and look at the little babies going into the water. They will hold their parents' hands or run over to be near their parents for a little reassurance. Finally, children request explanations as a way of responding to their fears. Sometimes these requests include questions about what makes wind, what causes darkness, whether monsters come out at night. These questions are a sign that children are almost ready to cope on their own.

Responding to requests begins with occasional refusal (running away, crying, whining, kicking) at the immature end of the continuum and ends in the mature ability to anticipate requests without even being told. Steps in between include learning to pay attention to parental requests, accepting requests because of the realization that it pleases the parents and brings good results, and then responding willingly to parental requests because of the pleasure the child receives from being pleasant and helpful. It is at this point that children become active helpers, wanting to help with whatever we are doing, such as setting the dinner table, drying dishes, dusting furniture, shopping, feeding the pets. They ask to help us because they receive great pleasure from being useful and appreciated.

Dealing with frustrations begins with crying, screaming, and fighting because of helplessness and dependency. Children start out unaware of ways to handle negative emotions caused by frustration. At the other end of the continuum, positive behavior in the face of frustration comes naturally because children are no longer thinking only of themselves and have learned to consider other possible responses to frustration. As children begin learning to deal with frustration, they first begin to rec-

ognize their negative emotions and make small attempts to deal with them such as crying less, stopping their pouting when reminded, beginning to share, getting along for small periods of time without their parents. Then they begin to deal with their negative emotions independently, and after that they begin learning more ways of channeling their emotions positively such as sharing, remaining cheerful, trying to make others happy.

Socially acceptable behavior has at one end of the continuum such socially unacceptable behavior as screaming, crying, jumping up and down, holding one's breath, throwing things. At the other end of the continuum is the positive, acceptable behavior of children sensitively concerned with how others react to their behavior. They want to be socially accepted by everyone and so behave accordingly. In moving from unacceptable to acceptable social behavior, the major steps children take over a period of three or four years are those of beginning to be aware of unacceptable behavior, beginning acceptable behavior, and then broadening acceptable behavior.

Becoming aware of unacceptable behavior means that children continue with negative behavior, such as crying, whining, or running away but their behavior is less extreme and uncontrolled because they are beginning to recognize approval and disapproval. Approval, especially by parents, begins to have importance. Acceptable behavior gradually begins, but not all at once and not on an even basis. Anger and other negative emotions still prevail every so often, but gradually the child begins to learn how to behave properly even when he would rather not; bit by bit acceptable behavior increases.

Developing imagination in play begins with action play, in which children try new activities simply for sheer enjoyment. They do not respond to direction very much, do not have any desire to do things correctly, and seem to be very haphazard about what they do. Next they begin to imitate and parrot what they see and hear. This is followed by make-believe play, and then fantasy play, and finally reality play. In reality play, which is highly mature for six year olds, details must be realistic. Dollhouses need pots and pans; people in play fantasies must speak the way real people speak. Children by this time love to play the parts of everyone, and they try hard to play them correctly. People, events, and things have become very, very interesting.

Summary

Childhood is a stage in human development which technically refers to the years between six and twelve but which loosely used refers to infancy, childhood, and adolescence. During the first thirty months of the infant's life, there occurs dramatic development of mouth-eye coordination, of the capacity for manipulation, of language, and of motor (muscle) abilities. Infants also develop in purposeful learning of skills, completing tasks, coping with fears, responding to requests, dealing with frustrations, acquiring socially acceptable behavior, and developing imagination in play. These developments add up to emotional growth. They form the foundation upon which all the rest of the child's emotional life will be lived.

CHAPTER TWO: Childhood

Children from about the age of six through twelve are subjected to what Taibi Kahler (a therapist and researcher who is expanding Transactional Analysis theory and methods) calls five basic driver commands. These *drivers* (commands) are the five categories into which nearly all parental injunctions and directions to their children could be sorted. They are the commands to:

> Be perfect,
> Please me,
> Hurry up,
> Try hard,
> Be strong.

These five categories of commands are the main content of the messages children receive from their parents. Parents give these commands in order to train their children. So, too, do teachers, coaches, scout leaders, and other group leaders. The child is urged to develop good habits of performance and character for future use. The commands act as *drivers* in the sense that they drive the child to ever greater efforts, while convincing the child that he or she is not OK unless performance levels are somehow satisfactorily achieved.

As the child grows into adulthood, one or another command becomes dominant and drives the person into negative conclusions about self whenever the command is in force. Thus, adults who try to be perfect feel bad because they are not perfect; adults who try to please others feel as though they are somehow failing since they have not pleased others sufficiently. The role which *drivers* play in the emotional development of children cannot be overestimated, since they are built into the emotional makeup of each child for the rest of life.

Be Perfect

"Be perfect" commands range over a host of child concerns. Parents and teachers tell children to be perfect with regard to grades at school, for example, by indicating that A is perfect while B is less than perfect and C is average. An A immediately becomes the goal to be striven for, as though the students who achieve an A are perfect; however, once achieving an A, the student is urged to do A+ work and to get even more A's in ever more subjects. Thus, those students who do not receive A's, as well as those who do, are both given to understand that while they must strive to be perfect, they are not perfect. When being perfect is present as the

norm or goal, nobody can feel good.

"Be perfect" messages abound all around children. Perfect attendance records, for example, are held up as a goal at many schools. Those children who attend school every day without ever being tardy are awarded citations. All the other students are then expected to emulate them. Perfect winning records, no-loss seasons, perfect games, flawless defenses, and perfect plays are held up as ideals on many little league, soccer, football, and bowling teams beginning as early as T-ball. Even through the movies and television, children are presented with the concepts of perfect love, perfect marriages, and ideal matches. Sainthood, perfect sanctity, is sometimes presented as what each of us should strive for.

"Be perfect" applies wherever competition is fostered, for to win is presented as better than losing, and to always win is presented as better than winning occasionally. Golfers who are afflicted with the *"be perfect"* driver know that no score is ever low enough, that perfection is never achieved. The nagging feelings about self that *"be perfect"* commands bring include feelings of depression, anger at self, poor opinion of one's self, hostility, resentment, sullenness, jealousy, feelings of not being appreciated, and a sense of not being loved.

Please Me

The *"please me"* driver, for some transactional analysis theorists, is the natural psychological condition of all children, since every child is in the situation of needing and wanting to please his parents and other adults. However, like the *"be perfect"* commands, the *"please me"* commands seem to dominate only some children and to become the most frequent driver in adulthood only for some persons.

Parents often use their being pleased as a reward or incentive for their children to perform well in sports, in school, or at home. "Positive reenforcement," for example, includes the use of parental or adult approval for those behaviors of the child which are desired. The idea is that the parental pleasure with the child becomes a kind of bait for which the child performs increasingly to gain ever more approval.

Children will grow and develop emotionally, it is true, from approval, since approval becomes the basis for ultimately deciding that they are OK and should accept or approve of themselves (healthy self-concept). Upon these feelings of self-esteem are based all further relationships, the ability to love others and form friendships, and general emotional stability. Those who cannot approve of themselves and who receive very little approval from their parents often become insecure, fearful, nervous, and lacking in assertiveness and self assurance.

However, those children in whom the *"please me"* commands take root too deeply will go the other way, trying ever harder to please others, with an increasing sense that no matter how hard they work to please their parents and others, they are still falling short and are, therefore, not OK. Not OK can mean different things, such as unloved, not worthy, guilty, likely to fail, not trustworthy, not respected, no good. It is the basis for some children concluding that their parents do not love them but are only pretending to be loving.

The *"please me"* commands and expectations are most vicious when they lead the child to conclude that the parents' love is based upon what the child does or achieves, rather than upon what the child is. Even those who love their children for what they are rather than for what they do can instill a sense of "you are not pleasing me sufficiently" by stressing the development of certain character traits, as though the child would be truly lovable only if he or she were to possess the desirable character traits. Some parents let their children know that they had hoped for a child of the opposite sex—a clear indication to the child in such a situation that he or she can never truly please the parents.

Hurry Up

"Hurry up" commands often come from over-intense parents and teachers, although not always. Children are urged to hustle around base paths, to swim faster in swim meets, to think faster in spelling bees, to go to bed quicker when it is late, to do their homework more rapidly, to hurry up and take their turn in games, to think faster when asked questions, and so forth. One of the most important things for teachers of kindergarten and first grade students is having patience and listening to what children are saying. All children want to tell the teacher what happened at home over the weekend, what happened to their pets, how they cut their finger. Every tale is told slowly, with detail, commanding the teacher's undivided and lengthy attention, as though the student were the only child in class. Lit-

tle children do not have the sense of urgency which keeps us adults eyeing the clock and getting nervous towards quitting time. Those children whose parents and adult figures manage to drum in a sense of *"hurry up"* will begin to feel inadequate, in that they can never hurry up sufficiently. Hyperactivity, guilt, shame, embarrassment, stuttering, hesitation, confusion, a sense of inadequacy, and feelings of greater determination and striving will result.

The *"hurry up"* driver is very real in the adult world. It is probably inevitable that our children will feel us responding to the pressure of this command. Starting time at work is just not going to change; getting to church on time remains a must. Hurrying to get to appointments and social occasions will always give rise to some pressure within the household. While our lives as adults and as children are regulated by schedules, starting times, quitting times, and urgent demands to meet the pace, what is within our control is the recognition that these are external commands. Our *worth* is in no way at stake, only our performance. It is possible to be late or slow and still be OK as a human being: that is the perspective that makes the difference.

Try Hard

Children are literally bombarded day and night with *"try hard"* messages, beginning with toilet training and continuing all the way into marriage where they are urged to try harder as a spouse, lover, and parent. *"Try hard"* seems to be the creed of our culture. Those who slack off are branded as poor sports, as letting down the team, as slow or non-motivated students, as poor employees, as poor risks for promotion, as unlikely to succeed. Not to try hard becomes a "naughty" during childhood. Most parents turn on the broadcasts of trying hard full blast, assuming that this is the type of encouragement their child needs. Of course, it is perfectly true that children need to try hard at what they do, and that trying hard is an important aspect of most tasks which life will present. The danger of this exhortation, however, is that children will assume it is their trying hard which pleases us and which makes them good in our eyes as parents. When such is their assumption, they will try ever harder and harder, since they wish to please their parents ever more and more, and since they want ever more and more assurances that they are indeed lovable and good.

"Try hard" is an especially important element in children's organized sports. Coaches seek to build character as well as athletic skills in those they coach. Trying hard is a very important aspect of athletic endeavor and character. The danger in this, however, is that children do not always realize when they have tried hard enough. In fact, they are often given to understand that they have not tried hard enough even when they have given a good effort. Sometimes *"try hard"* adults become coaches, adding a great deal more emotional punch to the endeavor than children can handle. A coach hit his own child for a poor performance, in a scene from the movie *Bad News Bears*. Children very quickly conclude from treatment of this sort that there is something wrong with them as a person. Parental injunctions to try hard for the team often reinforce such a conclusion. Parents feel they are being supportive to coaches in "motivating" their children and praising them for extra special efforts. What we as adults see as encouragement, however, can be much more than encouragement for children. Back of our urgings to our children can sometimes lie the thought, "If only I had tried harder when I was a child." This vicarious identification with our children's situation makes for trouble in our children as they grow into adulthood and become *"try harders."*

The adult who retains the *"try hard"* command as his or her chief motivation may become a compulsive worker, a worried producer, a distraught toiler.

Work will not be a joy but a battle; results will not tend to matter so much as the effort expended, the overtime hours given, the heroic sacrifices rendered along the way. This person will tend to prove loyalty through heroic, sacrificial work, through volunteering for extra tasks, through joining in and putting the old shoulder to every wheel that comes along.

Emotions which trying hard gives rise to in children are, like those related to the other *drivers*, both good and bad, positive and negative. The positive feelings of commitment to a task, perseverance, determination, control, self-reliance, and self-directedness are good. They enable the child to continue onward with the development of mouth-eyes, muscle, and other forms of development through the doing of tasks. They also help develop feelings of security, of being loved, and of being useful. Completion of tasks, learning of new skills, coping with fear, dealing with frustration, responding to requests, and developing socially acceptable behavior are all greatly aided by the will to try hard.

On the negative side, if the child is made to feel that he or she will be loved and will, indeed, be lovable only in proportion to trying hard, then the negative implication conveyed will be that in and of self the child is not lovable, not good enough to be accepted, not OK. It is this negative conclusion which will become the *driver* in later life, pushing the person to try ever harder, from the emotionally held conviction that only in trying does one achieve OKness. Put bluntly, the negative side of the *"hurry up"* commands, like that of the other four driver commands, is rejection.

Drivers and Their Consequences

Signal (Driver/Command)	Reasoning	Conclusion
Be Perfect	Or you will not be OK. BUT I'm not perfect	I'm not OK.
Please Me	Or you will not be OK. BUT I haven't pleased you	I'm not OK.
Hurry Up	Or you will not be OK. BUT I haven't hurried enough	I'm not OK.
Try Hard	Or you will not be OK. BUT I haven't tried hard enough	I'm not OK.
Be Strong	Or you will not be OK. BUT I haven't been strong enough	I'm not OK.

Be Strong

"Be strong" commands are sometimes given children with reference to the physical. That is, children are urged to be strong by developing more muscles, going into athletic training, and doing body-building exercises. More often, however, the *"be strong"* commands which flow almost spontaneously towards most children both at home and elsewhere have to do with emotional strength. Usually, those who give the commands misunderstand emotional strength assuming that it is almost identical with emotional non-expressiveness. Thus,

little children are urged to be "big little boys and girls and not cry" when Mommy abandons them at the day care center or nursery. They are praised for not crying when they are hurt, for not crying when they are disappointed, for not crying when we do not have time to play with them, cuddle them, rock them, put them to bed, read to them, talk to them, eat with them, or be with them. They are praised for not saying how they feel unless their feelings are happy and expressed with great brevity.

Teachers and day care workers often separate children who are fighting by punishing or reprimanding them for being angry—as though it were wrong to be angry and even more wrong to express such feelings. Children in social settings are increasingly allowed only to smile and "be nice." When they are angry, sad, resentful, feeling wronged, or otherwise down, they must leave the room, be by themselves, apologize, or fake being happy. Such adult supervision constitutes a command to *"be strong."* In boys this often is interpreted to mean that men do not cry and do not show emotion, and that any emotion which they do feel (and are not supposed or allowed to express) is also bad, unmasculine, weak, something to be feared and ashamed of feeling.

In girls, when *"be strong"* messages are given too often and taken too seriously, the conclusion sometimes drawn is that women are weak and emotions are the reason women are weak.

The Pyramid of Human Needs

Many people are familiar with the pyramid of

human needs. This concept was developed by Abraham Maslow and is widely referred to as a classic statement of the five categories of needs all humans experience every day. The pyramid, as seen in the illustration, indicates that the widest or greatest category of needs is that of the physiological. These are the needs which the infant works so hard to address through eating and sleeping, as well as through the various kinds of development described in Chapter One.

The next greatest level of needs, that of the emotional or psychological, are the needs which older children in the two- to six-year-old age range work at with such vigor.

The next two levels, loving and esteem, are the areas which are the focus of what is going on when driver commands are given, received, and processed. The child is trying always to love the parents, a natural and ever present, ever growing desire expressed in many different ways. When the parent expresses a driver command, whether it be the actual words, "be perfect, please me, hurry up, try hard, be strong," or a message that could be reduced to one of these phrases, the child hears a way in which the parent wishes to be loved.

It is loving and being loved that are the basis for self esteem and which allow us to give esteem to others in a healthy way. Esteem for somebody else on the basis that they are good, OK, wonderful but I am no good, not OK, not wonderful is not healthy. So what is critical in driver commands and the resultant behavior, especially during childhood, is the manner, the degree, and the amount of love which the child will be expected and allowed to give the

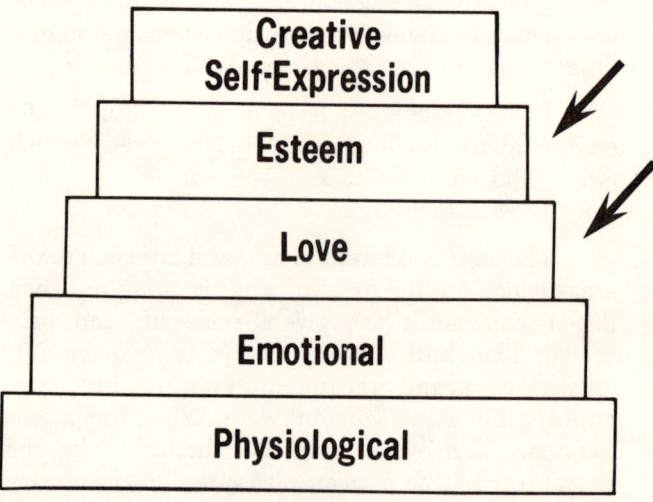

parent; also, whether the parent will love the child regardless of performance or on the basis of performance.

To the degree that the parent loves the child on the basis of performance, the child will likely learn to value himself or herself only or mostly in terms of performance. This conclusion would also mean that upon growing older, the child will find one or another of the drivers to be dominant and active in much of his or her behavior even when the parents have stopped issuing driver commands. Underneath it all will be an increasing sense of no self-worth, despair, despondency, depression, feelings of not OKness in one form or another.

To the degree that the parent loves the child not on the basis of performance but simply for being, the child will grow older feeling free to be, feeling good about self, acting and performing realistically in the here and now rather than on the basis of voices from the past or like a driven person. Underneath it all will be a profound sense of self-worth, high self-esteem as well as high esteem for others, a sense of peace and security, and emotional happiness that radiates from within.

CHAPTER THREE: Adolescence

One of the French cynics who doubted everything including life after death is supposed to have gathered his friends around his bedside as he lay dying. He remarked to them, when they had all assembled, "Now we draw the curtain on the great farce and begin the eternal perhaps." The time of adolescence, especially during the teen years, is the beginning of a great perhaps, too, with the "perhaps" referring to whether one is lovable.

Self-esteem comes into question for the first time in a serious way. The teenager seriously begins to place a question mark directly over his value, worth, and beauty as a person. That is, the teenager begins to wonder, "Am I lovable?" The great perhaps is that "Perhaps I am not lovable." Variations of this great perhaps include the possibilities that

The Adolescent's Search for Self Focuses Critically on the Need for Esteem

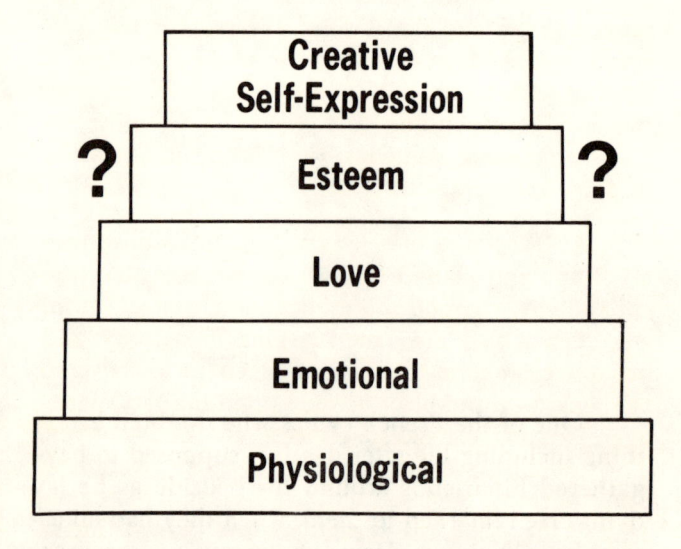

| Creative Self-Expression |
| Esteem |
| Love |
| Emotional |
| Physiological |

perhaps my parents love me only out of duty, that my friends love me only from a distance, and that if anyone were to get truly close and know me as I know myself, they would find me repulsive rather than lovable and attractive. Other variations include the ideas that those who love me are saying they love me only out of kindness or sympathy; that love is being given to encourage me in much the same way that coaches would praise a slow or clumsy player for trying hard to improve; that God, when he loves me, is only being merciful and condescending.

Self is a very important part of our emotional makeup. Our entire emotional life rises and falls with our concept of self. Self-esteem is part of our self-concept, self-image, or self-regard, for it is the value we place upon what we regard ourselves to be. In this sense, during infancy and childhood our self-regard grows and develops in the various ways already described, especially in the seven core areas of dealing with frustration, coping with fear, learning new skills, responding to requests, developing socially acceptable behavior, developing imagination in play, and completing tasks.

As awareness of self as a person distinct from all others and made up of all the various qualities, capabilities, characteristics, behavior patterns, and emotions which are "me" begins to solidify and become clear to me in the early teenage years, I, so to speak, begin to place a value upon the total package. This value is what is meant by "self-esteem." The lower I place the value on myself in relation to other persons, the lower my self-esteem. The higher I place the value, the greater my self-esteem. There are very, very few adolescents walking this earth with self-esteem that is too high. Suicide is very frequent among teenagers. Even more frequent is swaggering. Psychological swaggering is characterized by boasting, strutting, putting on airs, false fronts, pretense of strength and self reliance. Inside, the swaggerer is afraid, discouraged, hollow, and worried. He or she is fearful that inadequacies will be found out, that friends will mock, and that other forms of disaster will strike at any time.

The doubts and struggles about self-esteem begin in earnest with the beginning of adolescence, the start of the teenage years. But they by no means end with the end of the teenage years. For many, many people, self-esteem is never achieved, and for such people the struggle is still in progress even on their deathbed.

"Normal" psychological development would include the development of high self-esteem by the late thirties for women and by the early forties for men. Mature self-esteem helps make for mature friendships and relationships, for when we value ourselves highly we are able to trust others to do the same. Their praise does not appear to be flattery and encouragement, but can be taken as the truth. Humility, at such a point, is finally understood as acceptance of the truth about oneself, rather than as some sort of embarrassment about accepting praise. Humility and truth equate in this respect.

Inward-Outward: Self or Others?

Another way to think of emotional development during adolescence would be to visualize the first eighteen years of life as an inward-outward journey in relation to self: inward when self-centered and outward when other-centered.

The baby is born at the most self-centered point in the journey, for the baby does not know that others exist. As the baby learns to differentiate himself from others, there begins a slowly growing interest in others that moves from awareness to interest to fascination. The baby enters life as though he were the center of the universe, for all the adults hover about and revolve around him and his needs. Gradually he changes from being the center of attention to becoming a spectator or participant in

The Focus of the Child in Social Relationships

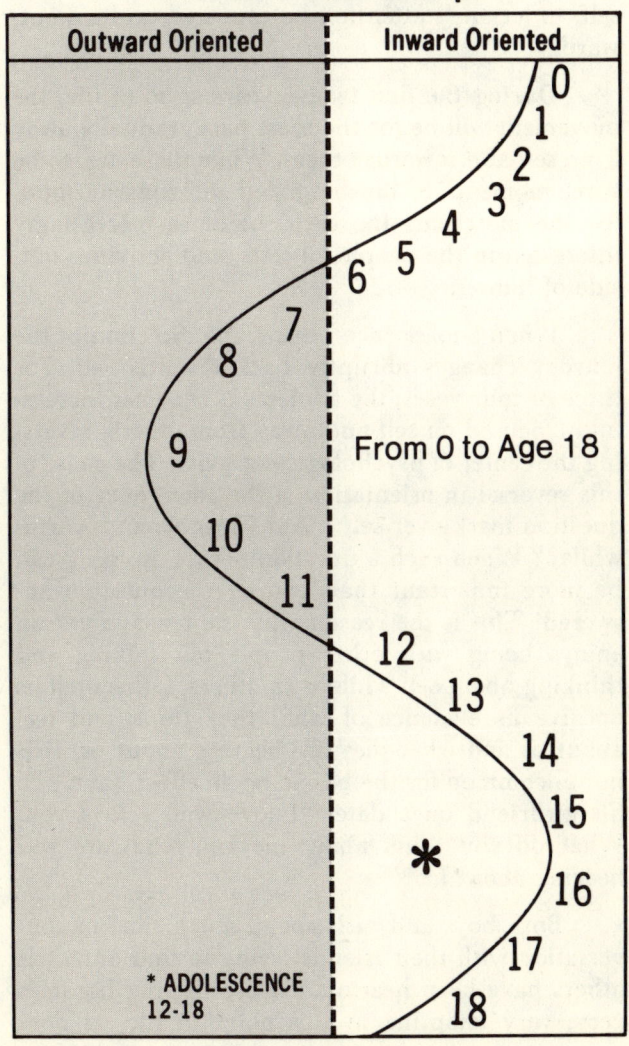

Outward Oriented	Inward Oriented

From 0 to Age 18

* ADOLESCENCE
12-18

somebody else's show! He likes to watch and learn because other people and things are so interesting! To be interested is to be caught up outside of one's self, to let one's attention be captured, to turn outward.

During the first twelve years or so of life, the movement will be for the most part gradually away from self and towards others. While there are, to be sure, moments of blushing and self-consciousness, for the most part the child becomes increasingly interested in the people, objects, and activities outside of himself.

When adolescence begins, the direction of the journey changes abruptly back towards self. For three or four years, the adolescent becomes increasingly focused on self and away from others, reversing the center of psychological gravity. The cause of this reversal in orientation is the emergence of the question mark over self: "Am I lovable and worthwhile?" When such a question occurs, nothing can be more important than getting the question answered! This is the reason why the teenage person enjoys being with other people but talking and thinking about self while with others. Others tell us or give us evidence of what they think and feel about us and what they are hearing about us. It is not uncommon for the boy to be, in effect, saying to his girlfriend on a date, "I love you, I love you. What do you think about me and what are you hearing about me?"

Both boys and girls spend much time in conversation with their friends trying to find out what others have been hearing. Eavesdropping becomes very, very tempting at this point in life, as does

3 Ways of Looking at Adolescent Development

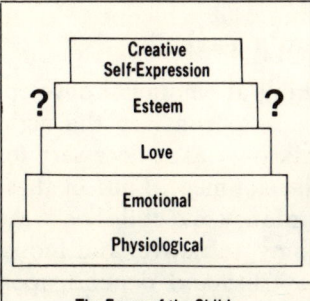

```
┌─────────────────────────┐
│   Creative              │
│   Self-Expression       │
│ ?   Esteem        ?     │
│     Love                │
│     Emotional           │
│     Physiological       │
└─────────────────────────┘
```

The Focus of the Child in Social Relationships

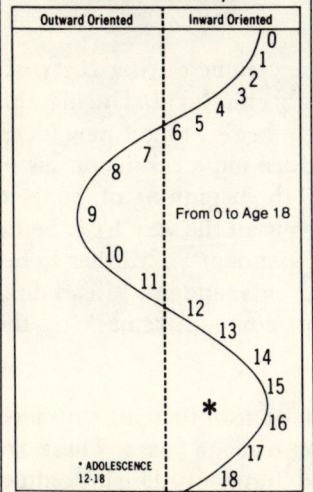

Outward Oriented | Inward Oriented

(Curve from 0 to 18)

From 0 to Age 18

* ADOLESCENCE 12-18

Erikson's "Tasks"

In Infancy, to Achieve:

Trust

In Childhood, to Gain:

1. Autonomy vs Shame, Guilt
2. Initiative vs Guilt
3. Industry vs Inferiority

In Adolescence, to Develop:

1. Identity ⇄ Devotion
   (Authority Crisis) Repudiation
   Moratorium
2. Intimacy vs Isolation

In Adulthood, to Gain:

1. Generativity
2. Integrity

reading other people's diaries, reports, letters, and notes for any and all references to self. To catch another person in an unguarded remark about me is to hear the truth, be it good or bad. And so, as a teenager, I will spend much effort trying to catch others in unguarded remarks about me, since one of my major concerns is to figure out the truth about myself and end the question mark.

Erikson's Tasks

Another way of looking at emotional development during adolescence is to consider the eight basic tasks which Erik Erikson sees as necessary for full human personality development. Four of these are accomplished during infancy and childhood: the achieving of trust, autonomy, initiative, and industry. The infant learns to trust and depend upon mother; later to differentiate self from others and to establish boundaries.

Initiative and industry come during the years from two onward through childhood. During this time the child increasingly begins to get new ideas, start new tasks, and produce more results on his or her own. From birth until the beginning of the teenage years, the person travels all the way from being completely passive and dependent on Mother to being completely active and independent. "I can do it myself" becomes the most common remark by the time of adolescence.

Two of Erikson's steps toward maturity need to be achieved during the teenage years. These are the steps of identity and intimacy. During adulthood the last two steps are achieved, that of generativity and integrity.

Identity becomes an important issue as the person becomes an adolescent. Identity is taken for granted until this time, mostly because until the teenage years there has not been enough introspection to be concerned about self-identity.

Just as the question mark over self during this period of life has to do with "Am I lovable?" so too it has to do with "Who am I?" Occasionally "Who am I?" literally questions whether or not I am adopted, whether my last name is my real name, whether my parents are my real natural parents. More often, though, the question has to do with "What kind of person do I wish to be, what do others see me as, how shall I define myself in contrast to all the others in my life?" It is not exactly that teenagers sit down and ask themselves these questions in just this form. The issues, however, boil down to these kinds of concerns.

Erikson sees three parts to the identity-finding process. The first part he calls "devotion," meaning that during this period of life each person needs to find something or someone of such great value as to compel loyalty, devotion, sacrifice, being caught up in and drawn out of one's self. A cause, a dream, a purpose in life begins to develop at this point. In proportion as I can give myself to something greater than myself, a sense of my own identity begins to come about!

The second part of the identity-finding process Erikson calls "repudiation," meaning that, while on the one hand I am giving myself to others and other causes greater than myself, at the same time I also begin to reject, pull away, draw back from people, especially those who are the authorities in my life, in order not to be dependent and in order to find out who I am. This process is one which will go on for the rest of life: each time I get too close or too involved with others, I will pull back in order to maintain a sense of my own boundaries. The third part of the identity-finding process Erikson calls "moratorium." This refers to that stage between childhood and adulthood in which what I do and what I commit myself to are not necessarily for the rest of my life. Moratorium is a kind of no-man's-land between what I was and what I will become.

The other step towards maturity which accompanies the working through of identity with its three parts of devotion, repudiation, and moratorium, is that of intimacy. Intimacy means the ability to join or fuse with another emotionally. This ability does not come until identity and boundaries have been well established. Intimacy can be very risky if our own identity and boundaries are weak. The risk is that in drawing close and sharing with another, we will not know where we end and the other begins. The uncomfortableness that follows such a situation has to do with not knowing whether to dominate or submit, not knowing how to please, experiencing feelings of suffocation and of being crowded, needing to get away, feeling irritated and threatened by others and yet unable to be alone without becoming depressed.

The first experience of intimacy, because intimacy is so powerful and threatening to self-identity, is usually embarrassing and confusing. People often stutter and blush on dates, finding it very difficult and awkward to express their feelings. Inti-

mate relationships, which are at bottom nothing more than friendship, always raise the questions of how strong is this friendship, what are my obligations, what am I supposed to do next? These questions arise because for the first time in my life I am no longer dependent upon my parents who settled all of those questions. Nor am I tied to my family and childhood friends where such issues were not serious. For the first time in my life I am an independent decision-maker, choosing my friends and in charge of my relationships. While adolescent relationships do not have the permanency of adult commitments, still they are serious and have implications for the future. This is the time when I begin to realize that yes, I am in charge of my life and yes, what I do with others is important. Responsibilities and commitments are not to be taken lightly.

Part of the thrill of falling in love and in having sex with another person is intimacy. There is great joy in physically abandoning one's self to another and in being literally one with another. But for the same reasons, there is fear in falling in love and in having sex with another person. To go that far with another person is to be committed and to be open, vulnerable, intertwined with another. The experience leaves both persons changed forever. For those who have little strength and a weak sense of self, the experience can be overwhelming and destructive. This is why readiness for marriage is so relative from person to person but a very important concern for all persons. To marry before one is ready in the sense of having become emotionally mature is to invite disaster.

Roller Coaster

Emotional life during adolescence is a roller coaster, up one minute, down the next. Depression follows high and highs follow depressions without rhyme or reason.

Adults have a regular emotional pattern of peaks and valleys. The distance from high to high in terms of days is constant for adults, just as the distance from low to low is constant. That is to say, if I am emotionally high every two weeks, I will be emotionally depressed with the same regularity following the highs. The intervals between highs and lows will, of course, vary from adult to adult and yet remain constant for any given person.

Depression makes bad news seem worse, while emotional highs make good news seem better. Adults can learn to anticipate their moods and not be surprised. Teenagers cannot anticipate their moods and are constantly surprised, sometimes fearing that they are going crazy. Emotional ups and downs in this irregular, even bizarre pattern are brought about during the teen years because of the hormonal imbalance due to sex changes, as well as the tremendous growth and changes going on physically and emotionally. These ups and downs make adolescence an emotional roller coaster. When the ride ends, early adulthood will have begun.

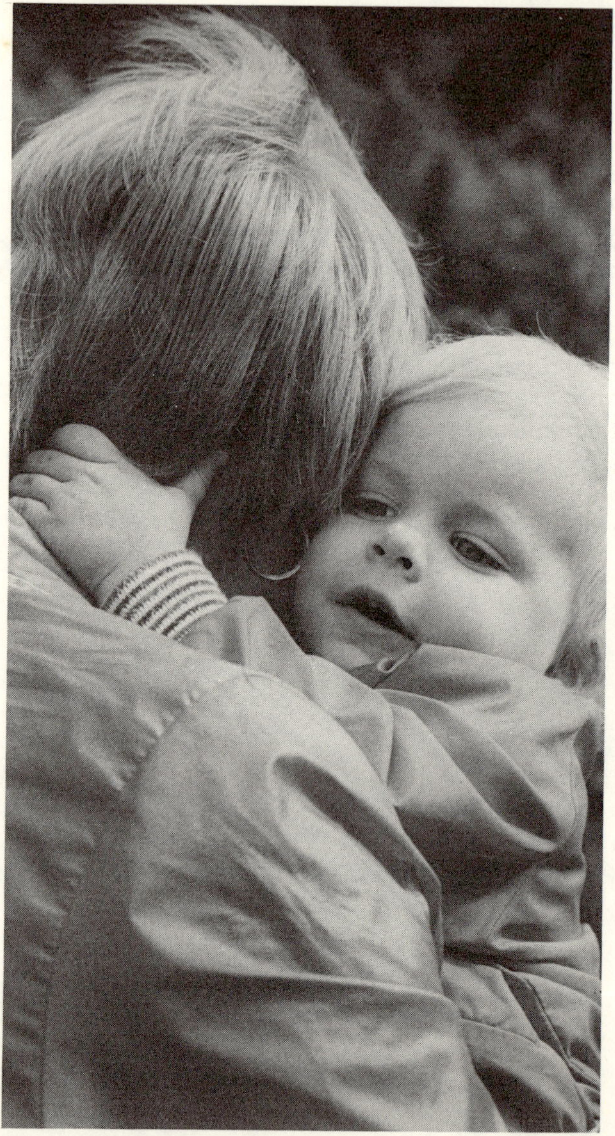

CHAPTER FOUR: When to Hug Infants

When do babies need us to hug them? All the time! Why? Because it makes them feel secure and loved. Love and security for people, *all* people, *all the time,* are like clean air and good health: we can never get too much. The baby is like a bottomless well when it comes to needing, wanting, and receiving love: he or she will take all we can give and still be ready for more, never running out of the capacity to accept love. We, however, are not like bottomless wells when it comes to giving love. We very quickly run out of the hugs we can give. And so the answer to how much love we give our babies is not determined by their needs, for they can take all we can give. The answer is determined by our limits. We need to hug-love our babies as much as we are able.

Our hugging can be random or it can be organized. I am very much in favor of organized, scheduled, planned hugging. Not that it isn't good to also hug and love our babies spontaneously! The difficulty about random hugging, however, is that it is truly haphazard. Some of us hug-love when we feel like it, when we remember to do it, when our babies demand it or seem to need it. Some of us "leave it to nature," believing that we will have the instinct to hug-love when the child needs it. Nothing could be further from the truth. The more our children need our hugs, the more put upon we feel, the more annoyed and frustrated, the more drained and irritable. Hugging babies in the many and various forms which they need is no easy undertaking. Witness the many mothers and fathers who volunteer to stay home and babysit the baby while their spouse goes out for a night off. A few hours later the babysitting mother or dad has become a nervous wreck, a raving maniac, a defeated warrior and vows never again.

Better to organize the hug-love effort. Such organization is best done based on both the actual needs of the baby and on our ability to give cheerfully. Three kinds of basic hug-hunger exist in babies: skin hunger, rhythm hunger, and place hunger. These are just made-up phrases to express three facets of security needs in infants: the security need to be touched frequently, the security need to hear soothing rhythms and sounds like those he or she experienced in the womb for nine months, and the security need of a stable, familiar, friendly place in which to sleep, eat, and play. The sense of security, *feeling safe,* is perhaps the most basic and important emotion of all, for without it all other emotions will be disordered and uncontrolled.

Skin Hunger

Skin hunger is the need for contact with another human. It is skin hunger that makes kissing and touching so enjoyable; it is skin hunger that makes dancing more than exercise, and sexual intercourse more than a physical function. It is skin hunger that makes all dying persons yearn to be held. While skin hunger is important and desirable from time to time during adulthood, it is a constant during childhood, especially during the first few years of life. Literally hugging a baby is the way to feed this hunger. Various other forms of hugging need also to be organized and planned if the hugs are to become solid nourishment.

One excellent way of building hugging into every day is to get a comfortable rocking chair and place it in a good spot—perhaps in the baby's room or in the TV room, or perhaps near the kitchen: some place in the house where everyone will be happy using the rocking chair to rock the baby or babies. Mother and Dad will then find it soothing rather than a chore to sit in the rocking chair and rock the baby, not only at feeding time but also while watching TV, carrying on conversations, or just relaxing.

If there are other children in the family, they too will use the rocking chair to rock the baby. Rocking chairs are wonderful, magical inventions: they soothe and comfort both the rocker and the rockee! If you have a rocking chair in your home, watch and see where the fighting and conflicts occur. Very rarely, if ever, will you see a fight of any kind going on around the rocking chair!

Another nice thing about rocking a baby is that, in order to do a good job of rocking, one must invariably touch a great percentage of the baby's skin. The body contact involved with rocking is at least half the body surface, be it the back side as in sitting and leaning back, or the front side as in clinging.

Walking the baby is nothing more than another form of rocking. It has all the same benefits, except that the walker can be more easily tired. Of course, on those days when Dad has worked long at the office and needs some exercise, walking the baby can be just what the doctor ordered. With a rocking chair handy, walking can lead to rocking and rocking can be the last step before putting the baby to bed for the night.

Another variation of hugging is rubbing. Babies love to have their backs rubbed. Rubbing of this kind feeds skin hunger and takes very little effort. Like rocking, it is as soothing for the one doing it as it is for the one receiving it. Back rubs can go on well into childhood, long after our children have become too big to walk and too grown up to enjoy being rocked. No coincidence that massage is becoming so popular in our culture at a time when anonymity and impersonal dealings prevail. Massage feeds skin hunger, a hunger which we all have, a hunger which can be satisfied both in receiving hugs and in giving hugs.

Another form of hugging is the kind given to help our babies and children regain control of their emotions. This form of hug might be thought of as the restraining or assisting hug. When the child is about to strike another child or the dog and we happen to be standing nearby, we instinctively reach out and stop the blow. It would only take another second to wrap our arms around the child, pick the child up, and draw the child close against our body. To do so would be to give a restraining hug. Most of the time this does not happen because the adult has not thought to do it.

Sometimes as adults we believe it is better to scream at the child, assuming that to show our anger about the imminent blow is to discipline the child. Anger does not restrain children or anyone else, for that matter. Nor does it feed skin hunger. Nor does it provide a sense of security, belonging, or being loved. This is no substitute for hugs. To use anger, retaliation, or punishment such as slaps and spankings is to make contact but with a reverse kind of effect. Instead of feeding the skin hunger and creating a sense of security, the negative words and blows on our children take away from them affection and security, creating more of a hunger. True, it may stop the blow they are about to strike, and true, it may stop the objectionable behavior, but at what price? By our negative, angry, violent discipline we create more of a vacuum in our children, more of a sense of insecurity, and thereby make objectionable behavior in them more likely in the long run, while getting ourselves upset in the process.

One of the most important situations in which to use restraining hugs is when the little ones pitch tantrums. It is so sad to see adults sitting or standing idly by while a baby or small child rolls around on the floor screaming, crying, and raging out of control. *Out of control* is the key element. Tantrums, whether they are being pitched by children, teenagers, or adults, only happen when a person is emotionally out of control. Usually it is anger that makes for a tantrum, but occasionally grief and especially frustration cause the same results.

To ignore the tantrum on grounds that it might spoil the child to "give the tantrum attention," is like saying that, even though the house is on fire, ignore it and do not pay it too much attention. The person in a tantrum is emotionally on fire, burning out of control, unable to control himself without help. When the tantrum is ignored, it will subside only as tiredness sets in, that is, it will run its course. While this is happening, the person suffering the tantrum becomes very frightened, even terrified, that the emotions cannot be controlled. Sometimes breathing becomes difficult or even stops, adding to the terror. A baby that stops breathing during a tantrum is not doing it to get attention!

Even worse than ignoring tantrums is to get angry and yell at the child in tantrum or to begin spanking the child. This adds our anger and hysteria to what is already an emotional bonfire, and is perhaps the cruelest thing an adult can do to a child! It is certainly one of the potentially most damaging things an adult can do to a child both emotionally and even physically.

It does no good to stand over a child bellowing, "Control yourself." If the child could control himself, he wouldn't be having the tantrum. No, a restraining hug is what is needed. We get the child in our arms, gently restraining the worst of the flailing and letting the child feel our body, our calm strength, our soothing touch, our steady breathing. We provide some external control and calm for the child until the child can regain control and begin calming down, to be followed by a period of rest, however brief. We help bring the emotional fire under control. That is when our child needs our hug the most!

Soft cuddly dolls, stuffed animals, favorite blankets, and pets also help feed skin hunger and provide another form of hugs for babies and children. The body contact from these is very significant. In the case of pets, the pets will give the children affection. Since babies and children need all they can get, they will not be too fussy about the source. How helpful to have the dog lying at our babies' feet licking them when we are too busy or harassed to hold the baby or play with our children!

The baby's favorite blanket becomes a kind of extension of Mother's loving warm embrace, for it represents a familiar and ever present, ever soothing presence from which the child can take comfort and good feelings. Pets, blankets, stuffed animals and dolls have the added feature of eliciting affection from the child. For the child to give affection and love are just as good for him as to receive hugs. No one has ever completely explained why this is so, and perhaps no one ever will be able to explain why it is, but it is. There is something about giving affection that affects the giver just as though he had received love rather than given it. And so when we are not there to hug our children, they can still do some hugging of their own if we will provide them with the few simple things needed to fill their world with pleasant, fluffy, smooth textures, objects of affection, and perhaps a devoted pet or two.

Rhythm Hunger

Rhythm hunger goes right along with skin hunger and is satisfied by being held, rocked, walked, rubbed in a steady rhythm. The first rhythm every baby hears is the steady thump-thump of his or her mother's heart for nine months. The next and most permanent rhythm the baby will hear is the sound of his own heart thump-thumping. This rhythm is both the most basic, most enduring, and most soothing of all rhythms, because it is present from the very beginning of our existence and because it is associated with life itself. Rhythm hunger, then, is the need for additional external soothing. It does not take very long for the need to be met, unlike skin hunger which is never entirely satisfied.

Another way of meeting rhythm hunger is to provide music for the baby and for all our children. Music is soothing to them, especially if the beat is discernible and the music not crashing loud. It is because of the rhythm that babies like to listen to the same familiar record over and over again. It is also this sense of rhythm that sometimes makes babies rock back and forth on their stomach or kick to a certain beat.

Place Hunger

Another facet of the need for security is what could be called place hunger. Place hunger is the need for a familiar, comfortable, safe place. Actually, babies have several such places. One is their crib and later their bed. Another is the room in which the bed resides. Another is the place where they eat, and another is their playing space or spaces in and around the house.

The crib is more than a mattress with bars on each side. It is an environment in which the baby spends most of each day for several years. Think of it that way and you will see the value in making it pleasant. Satisfying place hunger is a way of hugging the baby and at the same time facilitating the many other kinds of development going on during the first few years of life. For example, by placing a brightly colored mobile above the crib, you both provide a very pleasant addition to the baby's environment and also give the baby something to look at and follow with his eyes, a most important activity for strengthening and improving vision, an activity which needs to be done over and over for long hours and many days, weeks, months. While the baby lies in the crib sucking, his eyes will follow the mobile or other moving objects you have placed there, helping the baby learn to look and eat at the same time, a major accomplishment which leads to being able to put what he is looking at into his mouth.

Those moving objects also encourage the baby to reach, to touch, and to touch and look simultaneously, activities which are crucial for the development of coordination, especially that required to eventually be able to reach for food, grasp it, and put it into the mouth. Toys and rattles in the crib encourage the baby to stretch, to crawl, to look around for what is there. It is the effort of trying to move the body that gradually gives the baby strength and body control, a task which continues for years and years.

The crib and then eventually the bed are substitutes for the womb. Why shouldn't they be comfortable, pleasant, secure? Pleasantly snuggled in the crib, the baby becomes comfortable and secure, which feelings become the core of emotional stability and maturity later in life. We like our beds comfortable, pleasant, secure. All the more so is this important for the very young.

Many parents wonder about leaving their children in the dark at night when it is time for sleep. Babies are developing and changing, which means the policy to be pursued about darkness must also develop and change if it is to make sense.

At first, darkness does not bother most babies, since they have been in darkness for nine months and the darkness was soothing, familiar. At first it is light rather than darkness which bothers and even frightens babies. Even their sight for the first few weeks is blurry and light sensitive. Only moving objects can be seen, then gradually very distinct objects can be discerned, and then colored objects can be seen. For many months darkness is soothing rather than upsetting. Those babies that begin to cry when the lights go off are more likely crying at being left alone than at being afraid of the dark.

Eventually, however, many babies come to prefer what they can see in the light to what they cannot see in the dark, and at that point they will protest being put in the dark. This is a sign that they are beginning to find light more soothing than the dark, and is perfectly normal. What difference does it make to us whether our children fall asleep with the light on or the light off? What is important is that they fall asleep in as comfortable and soothing a fashion as possible, rather than with anger, frustration, and battles. Sleep, after all, *is* supposed to be pleasant and refreshing! Sometimes a dim light, one lamp, or a nightlight will do the trick, allowing some light without lighting up the rest of the household. Getting comfortable with the light and with the dark, especially at bedtime, is a big part of place hunger which all children experience.

Another important part of satisfying space hunger and at the same time encouraging the various kinds of development going on during the first few years of life is to provide babies with various sizes, shapes, and colors of blocks, clothespins, and other kinds of play objects that they can look at, pick up, throw, knock down, move, pile up, line up, chew on, pour out of, and feel. The easiest way to know which ones are the right ones for the baby's current stage of development is to place quite a variety nearby. The baby will concentrate on the ones he or she is most ready for. What a savings to us, the parents, who would otherwise need to spend a great deal of time and effort trying to determine what the baby was ready for next!

A final word about the activity which best combines all that we have been considering in this chapter in terms of skin hunger, rhythm hunger, and place hunger: what meets all of these hungers is the bathtub!

With warm soothing water, and the rhythmic

sounds of running and splashing water, the bathtub is a familiar friendly place which is much like the womb. Baths are wonderful for everyone; most wonderful for babies. Do not think of baths as primarily a matter of hygiene. They are much more than that. For many years children will love to play in their bath and look forward to it with great anticipation.

There are many kinds of skills which can be developed in the bathtub, perhaps the greatest of which is pouring. It doesn't make any difference if some water gets spilled in the tub—that is the beauty of it. What a perfect place to practice pouring! Pouring is one of those activities essential for the child before learning to read and write, because pouring stimulates brain-nerve-muscle coordination which eventually causes much more finger and eye control than would otherwise be the case. It takes a great deal of this kind of control in order to read and write. So bathtubs can be far more important than they look!

Many ideas have been suggested in this chapter, so there is a summary on page 63 for your convenience.

Summary of Chapter Four

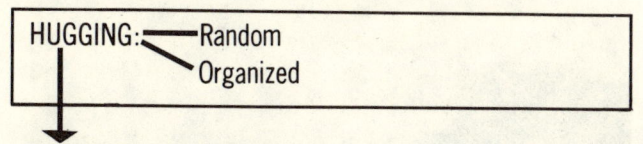

HUGGING: Random / Organized

↓

Feeds 3 Child "Hungers"

Skin Hunger	Rhythm Hunger	Place Hunger
Kiss	Heartbeat	Bed-Crib
Touch	Music	Room
Hold	Rocking	Play Space
Hug	Being Walked	Mobiles
Rock	Being Rubbed	Toys
Walk		Rattles
Rub		Blocks
Pat		Light
Restrain		Bathtub
Wrap		
Soft Cuddly Dolls		
Pets		
Blankets		
Fluffies		

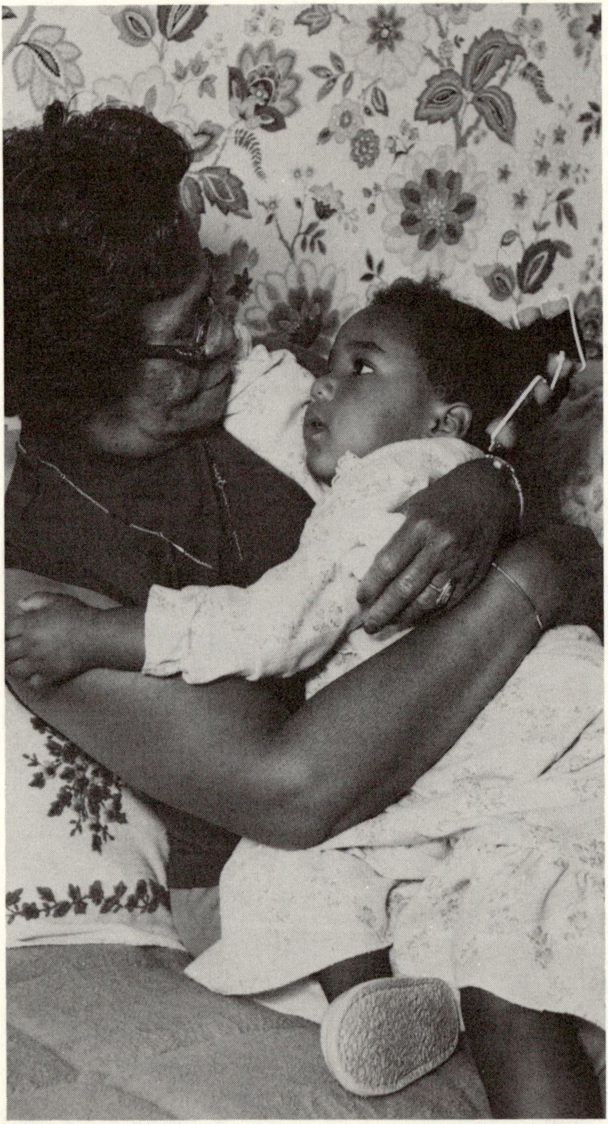

CHAPTER FIVE: When to Hug Children

Quality time is the best hug we can give our children. In giving our time, we give ourselves. We are what children need the most. Just as the needs of infancy were referred to as skin hunger, rhythm hunger, and place hunger, so the needs of childhood during the years of six through twelve can be thought of as psyche hunger.

Psyche hunger is the need to know that I am OK. The reason *driver commands* have such power is that they get at this very fundamental fear and need, the fear that I am not OK, and the need to be assured that I am OK and therefore that I am loved.

The temptation of parents during childhood is to praise their children for achievements. This is a natural and good temptation, based as it is on the thrill of watching our children progress and grow in skills. It is an instinct which ought to be honored. It is good to praise our children and to encourage them. What ought not be done, however, is to let our praise and love of our children hinge on their performance and their efforts. We must let them know how pleased we are with their performance, but we must also let them know that we love them, performance or no, success or no, effort or no.

That is where quality time comes in. Quality time is loving the person, not what the person has done or is doing. Quality time is listening and speaking directly to persons just because they are. Quality time is the gift of ourselves, for when we are bestowing quality time on someone, we cannot be doing anything else. Quality time is listening and looking to our little boy or girl when they ask a question or tell us what happened at school.

Quality time ends when I pick up the evening paper while my child is still talking to me. Quality time ends when I start saying, "Umm uh, oh is that so?" from behind the evening paper. Quality time ends when I start talking to my wife while my child is still talking to me. When I try to talk to my wife and listen to my child I deny both of them quality time.

A recent study in one of the midwest states revealed that, on the average, fathers spend far less quality time than mothers with their children, although neither mothers nor fathers spend much quality time with their children. Fathers in that state spend less than thirty quality minutes per week with their children, an average of less than four minutes per day!

Quality Time and Schedules

No great surprise that fathers do not spend much quality time with their children, considering the typical schedule of most families, especially during the school year. Father will get up and grab breakfast, dash out to the car, bus, or car pool in a desperate attempt not to be late for work. Somehow starting time at work always comes as such a surprise each morning, even though it has been the same time for years. Both parents and children try to sleep as late as possible each morning and still be on time for everything. The greater the panic to be on time, the less chance there will be that anybody gives anybody quality time. More likely what we give during the early morning rush are many negatives—much snarling, yelling, rushing around, commands to do this and do that, peevish requests, last minute instructions.

When Father does the driving of the children to school, he may feel even more harried. What starts out as assistance to children and to wife may often enough end up with Father appearing to be on the verge of a heart attack from the tension, rush, *"hurry up"* commands, and the fretting about traffic and possibly needed repairs on the car that always come to mind with the strange noises coming from under the hood on the way to school. (American cars are built to fail precisely between home and school, especially on days when both parents need the car and the other car is out of commission.)

Mother gives the children time in the morning, but not quality time. Her role may be that of the hatchet lady *i.e.* waking up the children who are lying in bed pretending to be asleep, reminding each child to take the right books to school, pointing out to all in the family that orange and green do not really go together in clothing, checking everyone for lunch money and AAH (anticipated arrival home). Her time is spent on the whole family, each morning often enough, but it is not time that is loving and undivided attention to anyone. Most neuroses in parents, especially in mothers, I believe, begin between the stove and the refrigerator at about 7:45 a.m. on weekdays. Deep feelings of inadequacy, resentfulness, tiredness, frayed nerves, and the futility of life seem to characterize this time, especially if not all in the family are morning persons to begin with.

In order to make sure that quality time will be given our children, schedules must be reckoned with. If mornings must be written off as a loss, and if no one will be home until nearly 5 p.m., quality time will need to be scheduled between 5 p.m. and bedtime. Within those hours, a host of other commitments may also intervene, such as scouting, little league, football, neighborhood games and friends, homework, religious education, television, baths, dinner, chores. The truth of the matter is that the American schedule is all filled up for both children and parents especially during the school year. Quality time needs to be scheduled for each person in the family each day, or it will never happen, despite all our good intentions and strong resolutions.

One starting place for quality time is the bedtime hug. That, certainly, is a time when everyone needs a hug. Because it is a quiet time and because it comes at the same time every night, it is a logical point at which to schedule some quality time.

Quality time at bedtime ought to include some conversation. Perhaps this is when we need to listen to each child telling about his day: what happened, how he feels, what he is wondering about. I know one man who gives his little girl one question to ask each night when she is in bed and all cuddled up ready to sleep. She has the right to ask him one question which he promises to answer. They record the question and answer on his tape recorder, which helps make this time special and which allows him to later hear himself talking to his own child. The act of pushing the recorder button serves to focus his attention each evening on his girl, reminding him to concentrate.

I give my children a little back rub each evening when they are almost asleep. Usually they tell me something they are thinking about, or ask one of those questions that come up just before they fall asleep and start dreaming in earnest.

Other starting points for scheduling quality time can be at the dinner table, just before or just after dinner, when each child says goodnight, on picking up the children from school, during snack times. In the winter time it might be when we sit down by the fire. Whenever quality time is going to be, it needs to be scheduled. Then any additional quality time can be so many extra hugs, a bonus so to speak.

There will be all kinds of opportunities as long as we have children around us, because what children want most from us is our attention. That is how we let them know they count. They want our attention because they *like* us and we mean something to them.

The requests for quality time come in an unending flow from morning to night. All we have to do is accept the invitation—whether it comes while we are driving along, sitting down to dinner, walking with our child, or whenever. Even listening to each person, one person at a time, during dinner can be quality time if we go with it.

What the Other Spouse Has Done

Quality time topics are not that many. One favorite topic is talking about the other spouse. Children talk to their mothers about what their father does at work, what he said to them yesterday, what he did with them when they went fishing, what happened when he was home babysitting. They talk to Dad about what Mother said to them when they were misbehaving, about what she meant when she was arguing with Dad, about when he met her and what it was like when they lived in some other city.

It is important for children to talk with one spouse about the other, for this assures children that their parents love them too, not just each other. Our little boy once remarked to my wife that when he grew up he was never going to leave home, just like his Mother and Dad! We were very complimented to think that he could not even imagine us as anything but Mother and Dad! He seemed so surprised to learn that we had once left home in order to marry and start his home! That is the kind of conversation that comes with quality time.

About School

Conversations about school are also very frequent during quality time. This is to be expected, since our children spend their day at school, undergoing not only the good experiences of school but also feeling pressure, challenges, social difficulties from time to time, and some failures. It is simply unrealistic to assume that the principal and teachers have total responsibility for what happens to our children at school.

One way we accept some of the responsibility is to listen to what they say about school. This means more than helping with homework, which in itself can be a quality hug; it means more than being a spectator at school events, more than driving our children to school, more than buying tickets and making contributions. It means *listening* to what our child says about school. Sometimes that means hearing out a struggle with an unjust, harsh, overbearing, or insensitive teacher. One of the demands of growing up is accepting what appears to be harsh treatment in a group setting. When our children talk to us about such matters, they are grappling. "Is it unjust? What should I do? Why me?" The age-old questions begin again in a new generation.

We listen and we answer gently. Not as the teacher's ally do we answer, but as one who loves our child. Not as one who tries to get the child to do yea and such, but as one who loves the child regardless of how the situation is handled. That's a hug: to see past the issue of struggle and into the soul of the child with loving acceptance. It is this acceptance, this love, which will ultimately teach our child the very lesson he needs most to learn: he is OK even if a teacher treats him harshly; he can be at peace with himself even when others are not. When we are at peace with our children they can be at peace. That is why they talk to us about school, especially when things are unsettled. We are their source of peace for these years until their peace can come from within.

Likewise, when things go well at school, our children need to hear our reactions, since we matter more to them than anyone else in their lives. It is one thing to be praised by a teacher or coach, something tremendously supportive to a child. But such praise needs to be affirmed by us. If we will listen when told about such praise, the praise earns interest. If we will not listen, the praise is counterfeited, negated, rendered far less effective.

About Friends

Quality hugs for children come mostly from other children. Much of each day is spent by a child doing something with another child or children—and the doing involves a great deal of talking and listening, far more than adults can give. Like teachers, however, friends mean only so much to a child, with parents either affirming these good experiences or negating them. We talk, as adults, to one another a great deal about our friends. What good would a friend be to our esteem and self worth were we to discover that everyone else we know considered this friend to be a fraud, a deceiver, an unworthy person? On the other hand, suppose a friend pays us a compliment and we learn from our spouse or some other person in our life that this friend is admired and regarded with warmth and affection: what a difference!

The more common situation with children is that their friends will lay *driver* commands upon them. "We don't want to play with you because you make us angry," *("please us")* or "Don't come at all if you are late," *("hurry up")* or "Weakies are not allowed" *("be strong")*. To be rejected by other children in the harsh, blunt manner that only children can use on one another is to be in considerable turmoil. That's when our children need a hug. They need to hear from us that their friends didn't really mean all those nasty remarks, that they are OK, that they do not need to perform up to expectations in order to be lovable.

Sometimes our children need to hear about our friendships, about some of the important moments we remember from our earlier days. They learn from our stories to place their own friendships in better perspective as a result. Another thing they learn is that we value them enough to share some of our experiences with them. It is this second kind of learning that frees our children from the awful grip of *driver* commands. We share our experiences with them because we love them—not because they tried hard or performed in some satisfactory manner. It is through this kind of hugging that our children become our friends.

About TV

Many estimates about the amount of TV watched by children have been made. Some estimates have it that a child will have seen 10,000 hours of television before entering first grade; that a child will see 14,000 killings on television before leaving eighth grade; that between grades one and eight students will spend more time watching television than they will spend in the classroom. Certainly, TV must be considered another member of the household, one more pervasive and influential than any of us truly realize. It would be helpful to clock the number of hours we spend watching TV with our children. These are potentially quality time opportunities, especially during commercials.

Commercials give us a chance to talk about

what we just saw, to mock what is silly, to observe what is worthy, to reflect on how we feel. What an easy time to put our arms around our children and talk with them! Once again, two messages are given. The first type of message has to do with the program, the information exchanged. But the second message has to do with our children being of more importance to us than what is happening on television, important enough to us that we will talk with them about what we are enjoying and sharing.

To Sum It All Up

Quality time is a hug, because when I give quality time I give myself. This can best be done by looking, listening, putting my arm around my child, being close, enjoying this other person, exchanging thoughts. The difficult thing is not so much doing it as finding time to do it and being alert to the signals which children send us from time to time each day inviting a quality response. Quality time is when I share a little of my head with my child, and when my child shares a little of his or her head with me. It's a magic time: the sharing of two heads causes the merging of two hearts and makes for one gigantic hug.

CHAPTER SIX: When to Hug Adolescents

How do we hug our teenagers? With strokes and by respecting boundaries. Strokes tell adolescent children that they are OK in our book. Our respecting boundaries which they have set around themselves tells them that we trust their judgement and are willing to let them be themselves. Strokes and boundaries: these are the two dominant needs of adolescents, and in proportion as these needs are met, identity and intimacy become possible. Intimacy and identity are the growth steps necessary to get from childhood into adulthood.

Strokes

Strokes can be both physical and nonphysical. When we rush up to our young son or daughter, throw our arms around him or her and say, "I love you," or, "How nice to see you!" or, "Welcome home," we are giving both physical strokes (the hug, arms around body) and nonphysical strokes (verbal greeting). Physical strokes are all forms of physical contact. Nonphysical strokes are all forms of nonphysical contact, such as words, gestures, written messages, facial expressions, gifts, and tokens of appreciation.

A stroke can be positive or negative. When it is positive, we call it affection. When it is negative, it takes away from the person and lowers self-esteem. A simple way to remember all this is to think of strokes as touching, whether the touching is literally touching or only symbolic. To stroke is to make contact with the other person. When we do so out of love and with affection, the stroke is positive. When we do so out of anger or some other negative feeling, the stroke is negative.

Positive strokes add to the person, negative strokes take away. Obviously, we all need as many positive strokes as we can possibly get. It is impossible to get too many positive strokes. Positive strokes are just like clean air: we can never get too much. Negative strokes are no good for anybody, and it is very easy to get too many of these. Even one is too many.

Adolescents have a special need for positive strokes, even more than persons of other ages. The reason for this, as we discussed in chapter three, is that a question mark slowly forms over the adolescent and within the adolescent's mind: "Am I lovable, am I any good?" Negative strokes encourage the answer, "No." Positive strokes encourage a much different conclusion: "Yes, I certainly am lovable because all kinds of people love me for real. This questioning of my own worth must be unwarranted."

The question mark is not resolved easily or quickly for any of us. Adolescence lasts a long time and reappears every so often for the rest of life. So positive strokes are very, very important. Without them, it is almost impossible to think well of ourselves. What are some of the ways we can stroke our teenagers?

Physical Strokes

The popular notion sometimes has it that teenagers are embarrassed by any display of parental affection. It is true that kissing our teenage children can be embarrassing and sometimes even emotionally damaging. But that does not mean we should treat our adolescent children like lepers and never again touch them!

Hugs are always in order; so are wrestling, holding hands, giving love taps, putting our arms around their shoulders, tapping, bumping, sitting side by side. Physical sports such as swimming, running, jogging, bicycling, playing ball, golf, and tennis also count as strokes. The point of physical stroking is to touch in some way, to be close, to make it clear that we like being close and like touching, feeding skin hunger. The teenager tends to wonder if maybe he or she is repulsive. Whenever physical strokes from parents decrease, teens almost always think that it is their own repulsiveness which causes it.

Some parents may experience sex-related fears

about physically stroking their children. The concern may be either way: that the child will read sexual overtones into what is happening or that the adult will be sexually tempted towards his or her own child. These are certainly legitimate, prudent concerns, and ought not to be overlooked. Modesty and prudence must always be the rule.

Each parent and each adolescent will, however, quite naturally find the happy medium between no physical stroking and so much stroking that sexual overtones begin to slip in. This happy medium will be different with each parent and child, and will tend to change often, but we are very adaptable creatures, we people. Our instincts can be trusted. We will know when too much is too much and when not enough is not enough. The point is, do not treat adolescents like lepers, for their very suspicion is that, socially and emotionally speaking, they are lepers.

Verbal Stroking

With little children, it is often difficult to get ourselves to talk to them less and touch them more. With big children, our difficulty often lies in getting ourselves to talk to them more. It is not so easy to talk to teenagers because they are smart enough to know when our heart isn't in it. It's a good deal easier just to consider adolescent people as "different" or moody, assume that they wouldn't be interested in what we have to say, and thereby escape talking to "them." Or even worse, it can quickly become habit to talk about and at adolescents, especially our own adolescent children.

When we talk about adolescents, we refer to

"them" with increasing regularity, as if "they" were somehow different, in a special category, apart from "us." "They" have done it again, "they" are a problem, an enigma, a concern, a headache, a source of comfort or pride, and somebody I talk about.

When I talk at adolescents, I give "you" messages with increasing regularity, as if "you" needed to be informed that "you" are to do your room, help your Mother, take care of your Father, do your chores, not come in late, in a word, as if "you" were not quite competent or were a robot into which I feed word signals in order to get desired results. One of the hidden but not-so-hidden results may be that "you" keep your distance, do not consider yourself to be anything near my equal, do not make any trouble for me, do as I tell you and not as I do, do not intrude into my life very much, do not relate to me in any way that might call for my relating to you as a genuine person in good standing.

Negative verbal strokes are often given as part of talking about or at adolescents. A negative verbal stroke is something said which is hurtful, which takes away from the person to whom or about whom it is said, which shows that we not only do not love the person but that we have bad feelings toward them.

St. James said that the person who did not sin with his mouth would be a perfect person. What, then, is the best way to avoid negative verbal strokes? The best way is to get into the habit of giving positive verbal strokes. When we fill up our speech with good things to and about others, there is no room left for bad things.

Good or positive verbal strokes are easy and fun. "Good morning," if said sincerely and not as a ritual, is a positive stroke. Compliments such as "That was a good job, nice going, I really appreciate what you are doing for me, thank you, how nice, what a pleasant surprise, you really make me feel good," take no effort to give but can be very good strokes to receive. This does not mean, of course, that we invent nice things to say when there is no justification for saying them. Rather, it means noticing what our adolescents are doing that is worthwhile. They are always doing more worthwhile things than we would think, simply because we do not pay enough attention.

To be a good verbal stroker means to enter into the life of the persons we love by noticing what they are doing, by listening to what is important to them, by sensing their concerns, and verbally acknowledging their efforts, their love, their goodness. It is a form of stroking to poke fun at others when the fun is genuine and not hurtful or sarcastic. To have fun and joke with one another is not only to notice the person but to give him or her credit for having a sense of humor. Tickling can be stroking.

Gestures and Gifts

The gesture is an important way of communicating, one which is quite popular in our country but in a negative sort of way. Gestures of contempt, defiance, anger, and vulgarity have become a way of life. They prove all over again how much effective communication can be achieved through gesture. Positive gestures, such as thumbs up, V for victory, clapping, cheering, and other gestures of encouragement and support can be just as effective for positive stroking, as can be facial expressions such as smiles, laughter, and grins.

Another form of "gesture" is the thoughtful act we do for others, the sensitive awareness we show in remembering what another person wanted, such as a ticket to a certain game, the car by such and such a time, a certain item of clothing, or a certain tool for some special job. These kinds of gestures show we hear and we care, and that is a stroke. Presents, in this sense, are a gesture of affection, very positive strokes, as long as presents are not used as bribes or in lieu of giving ourselves to our children in the form of our time, our emotional involvement, our listening, our being with, our getting involved.

Trips, ballgames, spontaneous horseplay, going swimming, fishing, hunting, hiking, backpacking, camping, bowling, or biking together with one or more of our teenage children count as giant strokes, gestures which say clearly that we prefer to be with our children rather than be alone or with other adults, at least for this outing, this trip, this adventure.

Boundaries

Boundaries and strokes are two very large needs for most adolescent persons. It is through strokes that he or she receives the good things others have to communicate; it implies letting down the barriers and boundaries, being open to others, letting others see inside and empathize. Boundaries serve just the opposite purpose: they keep other people out and keep me in, private, sealed off, alone with my feelings and thoughts.

Boundaries seem anti-social. When adolescents first begin to build up their boundaries, others in the family sometimes get alarmed or feel hurt and rejected. Actually, the firming up of boundaries serves a good purpose, because it is a means by which the person begins to define himself or herself, making it more clear where he or she ends and another person begins.

Boundaries are defined physically by little children, usually during the first several years of life. Two and three year olds will often feel their faces with their hands and then feel the face of a person near them. They are trying to determine where their face ends physically and where another's begins; they are trying to "get the feel" of their nose, their eyes, their mouth, their ears, and so forth, trying to imagine what they look like, how they compare to other people. This process of boundary determination in the physical order by little children helps them get a sense of themselves, the beginning of identity.

It is interesting to note that some of the physical boundary setting and getting acquainted with self still goes on during adolescence. The human body changes much more rapidly during adolescence than at any other time in life. It grows, enlarges, changes in hormone level, develops the external sex characteristics of enlarged breasts for girls and enlarging penis and scrotum for boys, as well as the secondary sexual characteristics of enlarged hips and pubic hair for girls, deepening voice, body hair, and whiskers for boys.

Clumsiness once again becomes a problem at this period of life because the body rapidly changes in size and proportion, thereby causing coordination problems. So there is considerable physical boundary re-examining and getting acquainted which is both necessary and healthy. But the emotional or personal boundary setting is even more important. The adolescent person must work hard to develop and maintain boundaries within which others will enter only by permission. Gone forever are the days of childhood when Mother, Dad, and others both in the family and outside could interact at will, could know what feelings and thoughts were on this person's inside even without asking, could enter emotionally, intellectually, socially into this person's thoughts or feelings and be right at home.

With adolescence all the entrances into the young person are checked over, so to speak, fortified, shored up, defended, guarded carefully, and closed often. It is through this process that the real adult person comes into being, that the adolescent finds himself and is able to claim himself as an adult, independent, not open to free invasion, able to stand and function independently of others.

Privacy, therefore, becomes a very important need of teenagers and pre-teenagers. Privacy means that I can have time, space, relationships, commitments, conversations, thoughts, dreams, and feelings of my own which I do not need to share with everyone or anyone in my family or elsewhere. It means that we, as parents, must concede our children at this point the right to tell us what they want us to know and not tell us what they do not want us to know—a very, very difficult form of trust indeed!

Privacy means a room, working space, and storage space that no one else will enter, observe, disturb, or share. It also means the ability to talk on the telephone without being overheard by *anyone ever*. Telephones are the objects of many battles in many families. They are expensive. Besides, we adults view telephones as practical communication tools, nothing more. "Why should our adolescent son or daughter need one of his or her very own?"

"Why should they need so much time on the phone? What is it they are hiding from us? What can possibly be so important about the telephone, and why all the fuss?" That is sometimes the adult point of view about the matter. But from the point of view of an adolescent, the telephone represents something by which very personal relationships, communications, conversations can be conducted. That is to say, it is one way in which I share myself with others. The thought that parents or other non-invited parties should listen in, overhear, eavesdrop, or be present to such conversations is just intolerable because it represents a violation of boundaries.

Boundaries go up around self, then, during adolescence. These boundaries include telephone conversations, the need for privacy, room, and space which can be called "mine." Guarded by these boundaries are my thoughts, my feelings, my friends, my fantasies, my self!

When boundaries are erected, maintained, enlarged, or defended by teenagers against us, their elders, this does not mean that we will never share again. Quite the contrary, it guarantees that we will be able to continue sharing ourselves with our children, because by having boundaries which they can control, they feel more secure and comfortable in dealing with us. Sharing with us will be done on their terms, which makes sharing possible!

Our role, then, as adults, when we see boundaries going up, is to observe them and see them as positive, constructive forces in the relationships we will continue to have with our children. Respect these boundaries, and all will go well, for the boundaries are a sign of further maturing in our children. Ultimately, these boundaries become the basis for achieving both identity and intimacy, the two tasks by which our children change from being children into being young men and women, just as we did.

As parents, giving strokes to our teenagers and honoring the new and changing boundaries which they erect are what make us feel old, not to mention panicky, insecure, angry, or otherwise uneasy. Emotional development at this point becomes *our* challenge as well as our children's challenge, for at this point we must once again grow up some more and start letting go. It is the letting go that makes us feel old and sad, even though we are not old and should be happy.

Bill Jacobs, in his paperback *Thank God for My Wife and Kid* compares this time in our lives as parents with teaching a person to ride a horse. There comes a time in learning to ride when the student must ride the horse and the instructor must stand by, waiting to see if the rider will fall off or sit the horse securely. To stand there and risk the student's falling is very, very difficult, but absolutely essential if the student is to become a rider in his or her own right. The student must learn to control the horse and make the horse respond to his will. That is what it means to be a rider.

Our children at this point in their lives are learning to control and direct themselves. They must ride in their own right for the rest of life, and we must begin learning to stand by and watch and hope and risk and care but let go—the supreme stroke!

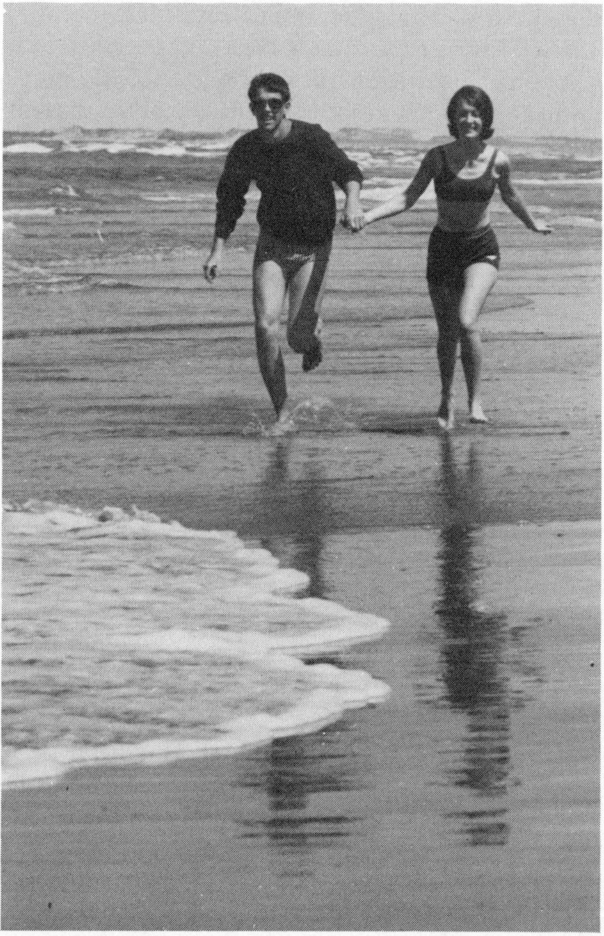

CHAPTER SEVEN: When to Hug the Kid that Lives within Each of Us

This little book has been all about children for six chapters. When to hug our child? That is the question. Always! That is the answer. We hug our child all the time, because that is when the child needs hugging. We do it in many different forms, responding to the needs and requests appropriate to each stage of growing up. As our teenagers start to become adults, we continue to hug and stroke them, but in ways that respect their new identity and new needs for intimacy. These new needs propel our children into adulthood and away from us as they search out new identities for themselves, new relationships, a life of their own. We hug them by supporting, trusting, honoring them.

But what about ourselves? Does the scenario end with us as the proud-sad parents standing at the gate tearfully waving fond farewell as our children journey alone into the future? Does the script have us spending the last fifty or sixty years of our lives in solitude, nursing memories, tearfully but bravely sacrificing ourselves to loneliness? There may well be fifty or sixty years ahead for us when our children are twenty-five or thirty years old, for life expectancy is already well into more than seventy years of age, and continues to rise.

Many adults carry around inner messages from their own upbringing, from novels and movies, and from advice they have garnered during their parenting days which would have them feel guilty for having fun. Parents are not supposed to have fun. After the children are grown, parents are supposed to settle down into drab old age, not have sex very much, not be kids themselves anymore, not do silly things, not laugh, not be young, not live, not be.

Transactional analysis theorists point out consistently that all of us, regardless of age, have a playful dimension which is very, very healthy and which ought not be bottled up if we are to be happy.

While our children are growing up we need this dimension. From it comes our fun, our sense of humor, our ability not to be grim all the time, our balance and perspective. But when our children grow up, we need this dimension even more, for it also serves to keep us young.

So, the last piece of advice I have for readers of these pages is "Play with the kid within you. Let that kid out and enjoy yourselves."

Throw some snowballs at your friends and at

your husband or wife. If you live where it is very hot all the time, throw some coconuts around at people once in awhile.

Have some pillow fights once in awhile and enjoy some good sex afterwards with your husband or wife whom you love.

Tickle people every chance you get. Make sure you get lots of chances.

Run in the surf a lot.

If you do not live near the surf, take lots of vacations where there is surf.

Go ice skating and roller skating every chance you get.

Do lots of fishing.

Swim and play stupid, fun games in the water.

Run through your garden or lawn sprinkler and let the neighbors see you doing it.

Squirt the neighbors with your garden hose.

Make funny faces and wisecracks to the postman.

Play a lot of golf, bridge, poker, or whatever games are your favorites.

Go out with your friends a lot.

Be spontaneous.

Let yourself be.

Thank God you are.

This chapter has deliberately been left uncompleted, because the rest of it is for you and your life. You finish this chapter with some jottings of your own about when *you* need a hug and about how you are going to get and give hugs for the rest of your life.

Happy hugging ...

Suggestions for Further Reading

Barber, Lucie and Peatling, John. *Scales of Self Regard.* Schenectady: Character Research Project, 1975.

Allows parents to measure and chart development of children ages 2 years to 6 years in the seven key areas of self-regard. Excellent.

[Character Research Project, 207 State St., Schenectady, NY 12305]

Elias, John L. *Psychology and Religious Education.* Bethlehem: Catechetical Communications, 1975.

Very useful summary of key psychological theorists.

[Catechetical Communications, 2499 Willow Park Rd., Bethlehem, PA 18017]

Levinson, Daniel J. *The Seasons of a Man's Life.* New York: Alfred A. Knopf, Inc., 1978.

Describes adult growth and overlapping stages of development. Much of Gail Sheehy's *Passages* is based upon research in this book.

Lignon, Ernest M.; Barber, Lucie; and Williams, Herman J. *Let Me Introduce Myself.* Schenectady: Character Research Project, 1976.

Text and workbook for observing and recording child development from birth to 30 months. Excellent.

Losoncy, Larry. *Religious Education and the Life Cycle.* Bethlehem: Catechetical Communications, 1977.

Shows how religious development occurs during the various stages of the life cycle, relating human development to religious-faith development, with suggestions for parents and teachers.

Powell, John. *Why Am I Afraid to Love?* Niles: Argus Communications, 1972.

Explores the possibilities and problems of loving, applying Transactional Analysis theory to everyday living and human relationships.

Powell, John. *Why Am I Afraid to Tell You Who I Am?* Niles: Argus Communications, 1969.

Applies Transactional Analysis theory to everyday living and human relationships, with an accent on love and communication.